-----HOW TO HAVE-----

MIND BLOWING

Engaging & Energizing

MEETINGS

From boring to interesting & effective meetings
using radiant thinking

MANEESH DUTT

NOTION PRESS

NOTION PRESS

India. Singapore. Malaysia.

ISBN 978-1-64324-815-8

Dedicated to all those who are truly interested in getting   the most out of organisational meetings but don't know how...

Contents

Introduction

Somewhere in my mid-40s after having worked in various organisations for over two decades, a quiet discontent brewing within me. My workplace was good but still I needed something new to re-energize myself. I guess this happens to a lot of us when we are looking for a change but still do not have the right amount of clarity about what one is looking for. I was slowly and daily getting entangled in this dilemma.

In the midst of all this like in any organisation, there were these never-ending meetings, which were routinely boring and added to my existing pain. On one such occasion, as I entered an empty conference room to attend yet another meeting, I discovered a book lying face down on the table. Being a book lover, my natural instinct prompted me to pick it up to discover it was "How to Mind Map" by Mr. Tony Buzan [1]. The subject was new to me and while waiting for the others to join the meeting, I started reading the book not realizing that I had stopped only after having completed it an hour or so later! Due to some stroke of luck, nobody had turned up for the scheduled meeting, and the only and probably my best meeting that happened was between me and that life changing book!

I started observing Mind Maps everywhere in nature, began experimenting with the concept in multiple situations and was really amazed by the results that I was getting. One area, which gave me particularly outstanding results using Mind Maps was in meetings. I realized it was so much easier for me to conduct and get engaging participation from everyone present in a meeting, all thanks to Mind Mapping.

This eventual success that I have had with Mind Maps in meetings and brainstorming sessions during my consultancy workshops as a freelancer has inspired me to write this Book. There are of course many other areas where Mind Maps can be applied (covered in my other books). I, however, believe, leveraging Mind Maps for organizational meetings can be singularly powerful to transform positively the outcome in every meeting in an organisation. And what's more, every organisation, either knowingly or unknowingly, is constantly looking for ways and means to make their meetings more fun and productive.

At the same time my experience tells me that given the fact that Mind Maps are a fundamentally different (but brain friendly) way of approaching a situation, people who get introduced to the concept still need a little more support and encouragement before they can move full steam using Mind Maps as a tool of choice for their meetings and more. Let me come back to this in a moment after looking at an entirely different example.

Let us say, one fine Sunday morning you are feeling unusually energetic and decide to do a bit of aerobics.

Towards the end you feel energized and in moments of happiness, you declare to yourself that you will do this every day now for the rest of your life! And what happens the next day? Well, every day is not a Sunday and the aerobics that felt like play yesterday may seem like climbing Mount Everest today. What happened? Very simply put, your desire or declaration to change in those happy moments was not enough to create a new habit, even though it may have seemed otherwise when you were in that blessed moment. And without the new habit, our life remains pretty much the same since we change not by what we do but by what we do daily! So, what is the way out?

The simple answer is we need a catalyst to help us make that change. And each one of us may have a different catalyst to motivate us. For doing aerobics daily, someone may get help by having an accountability partner, for others it could be a vision board, for some reading a book may be a big motivator and so on and so forth.

Now, this Book both introduces the concept of Mind Maps (for those entirely new to the subject) and then provides a plethora of ready to use templates for various situations, which act as a catalyst to help Managers and CEOs conduct more meaningful, engaging and Mind-blowing meetings using the power of radiant thinking. The organizational areas, which are addressed in this Book with the help of the ready to use templates are as follows:

- Goals Setting

- Decision Making
- Communication
- Planning
- Sales & Marketing
- Project Management
- Innovation

Once you get started with Mind Mapping, I can assure you that there will be no looking back! With that I sincerely hope and wish that this playbook, true to its name, helps transforms your boring meetings into mind blowing ones with the power of visual thinking via Mind Maps. Go forth and unleash your organization with this simple yet life changing tool.

1. Mind Mapping in Action

"I think it's very important to have a feedback loop, where you're constantly thinking about what you've done and how you could be doing it better. I think that's the single best piece of advice: constantly think about how you could be doing things better and questioning yourself."

- Elon Musk

I am a strong believer that the acid test and utility of any management tool or technique can be gauged by the scale of its application both at work as well as in personal life. So, though I had accidently stumbled upon the concept of Mind Maps in an office environment, my first inclination was to apply it to my personal front. And my first mind mapping client was my wife! When I broke the news that I wanted to teach her Mind Mapping, her immediate distrusting reaction was, "Is this one more management jargon of your's?" When my wife, however, learnt about Mind Mapping, to my surprise, she started discovering avenues on her own for applying Mind Maps in her consultancy work, teaching the kids, planning events, holidays and more.

The way my better half reacted to Mind Maps at first is potentially how many of us approach something new with scepticism until we get to taste the pudding. In this chapter, hence I plan to give you a taste of the pudding by sharing real life examples of Mind Mapping in an organisational context and in the subsequent chapters, we will look at steps for making effective Mind Maps, specifically using them in the context of meetings.

First of all, let us understand what a Mind Map is and how it can help.

A Mind Map is a visual thinking tool based on a radiant hierarchy, and in an organizational context, it helps broadly in two ways:

1) **Helps Compress large amount of existing information in a single page:** Activities such as making a summary of a large report, taking notes during a talk or even a meeting etc. all can be done more effectively using Mind Maps.

2) **Helps in creative thinking thus maximising ideas generation in various situations:** Ideas are the fuel for propelling an organisation onto a growth path. It is, therefore, imperative that organisations have necessary techniques at hand to tap individual and group creativity. Due to the brain friendly nature of Mind Mapping, which we will come to see shortly, it becomes easy and natural to generate ideas both at an individual level and as a group.

Now, information collation and ideas generation are the two most important pillars of any organisational meeting. Meetings become boring when there is an information overload and also when ideas are sought from the participants in a linear and traditional manner, which fail to tap the unique intelligence of the participating individuals in the meeting.

Let us look at a real-life example of each of the above applications to understand this power of Mind Mapping.

First, let us look at an example of how a large amount of information can be easily condensed in a single page or mind map. A Mind Map to this effect is shown in figure 1.1. This Mind Map captures the changes introduced by the Indian Health Authorities as a result of the introduction of a new set of Medical Device Rules, which superseded the previous one. The salient changes vis-à-vis the earlier guidelines are captured in this Mind Map. The source of this Mind Map is a document i.e. the Medical Device Rules comprising large amounts of "static" information. Similarly, there are a multitude of sources, which bombard us with heaps of information such as an article in a newspaper, a chapter of a book (or a book itself), a lecture, a video, a teleconference, etc. etc. Independent of the medium of the information source, it is always possible to condense and collate large information sets in the form of a Mind Map.

This was an example of a Mind Map for collecting information. Let us now look at another example for generating and collecting ideas.

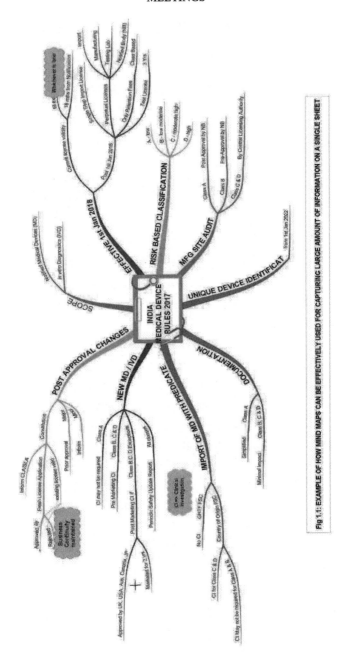

Fig 1.1: EXAMPLE OF HOW MIND MAPS CAN BE EFFECTIVELY USED FOR CAPTURING LARGE AMOUNT OF INFORMATION ON A SINGLE SHEET

As part of my consultancy, I was invited to do a brainstorming session with 30+ employees in an organisation, which was going through difficult times. The idea was to identify areas for improvements, which could help the management get the organisation back onto the path of recovery.

Now in a brainstorming session, it is very important that every participant is heard. So, my first step (after introducing the team to Mind Mapping) was to get the individual teams (4 teams of 6-8 participants each) to make their group Mind Maps (following a prescribed process, about which we will talk later) wherein thoughts and ideas could be captured in the comfort of smaller teams. After all the teams were ready with their Mind Maps, each of the teams began presenting their ideas for improvement, which were simultaneously captured by me on a Mind Map. The resultant Mind Map is presented in figure 1.2.

In effect, therefore, diverse ideas from 30+ participants grouped into four teams could easily be collected in less than an hour onto a single Mind Map in an extremely engaging manner. This is a lot of ideas being condensed in an easy to understand manner. This, of course, is just the first step in a longer process towards final identification of necessary actions for improvement. It is, however, really valuable data, which when stratified in the right way would lead to the right destination.

This was one example of how Mind Maps helped easily collect a variety of ideas from different people onto a

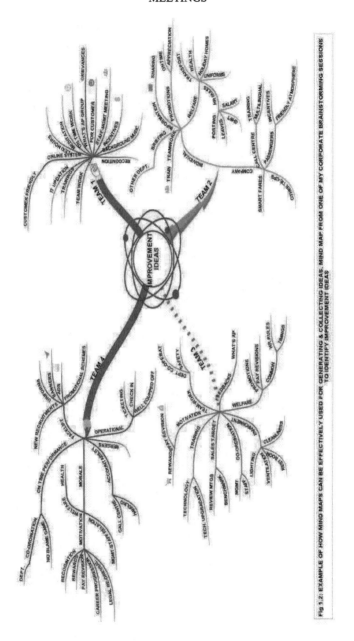

Fig 1.2: EXAMPLE OF HOW MIND MAPS CAN BE EFFECTIVELY USED FOR GENERATING & COLLECTING IDEAS. MIND MAP FROM ONE OF MY CORPORATE BRAINSTORMING SESSIONS TO IDENTIFY IMPROVEMENT IDEAS

single slate. It may appear, especially to someone new to Mind Mapping, that the output could have been achieved with linear or bullet point collation of the points. But this is not true since the brain friendly technique of Mind Mapping not only helps improve the quantity of ideas being generated but also the quality of ideas. More about this in a later chapter.

We have looked at two examples in this chapter: one for using Mind Maps in meetings for organising information and another one for creative ideas generation in a team. Though the focus of this Book is on using Mind Maps for meetings, as part of the process we must first learn how to make good individual Mind Maps. Hence in the next chapter, we look at steps for making effective Mind Maps.

2. Making Effective Mind Maps

"Creativity is the way I share my soul with the world."
- Brene Brown

Having looked at the two examples in the previous chapters, you would have probably understood to an extent how to make a Mind Map. On the face of it, Mind Maps may look deceptively simple to the point of undermining their immense potential.

It is, however, still important to familiarise ourselves with the steps for making effective hand drawn Mind Maps, which are based on extensive scientific research by Mr. Tony Buzan, inventor of Mind Maps. Once we become familiar with these steps, it would be easier for us to transition to a computer driven software for Mind Mapping.

The 7 steps to be followed for effective Mind Maps are as follows [2] :

1. We start at the centre of a blank page in a landscape layout and not portrait layout, which we ever so often do.

This allows the brain the freedom to spread out in all directions and to express itself more freely and naturally. Starting at the centre reinforces the radiant reality we see so often in Nature around us.

2. We use an IMAGE or PICTURE appropriate to the central idea to enhance imagination and focus. Putting down the picture we have in mind about the subject helps focus our thoughts better. It not only tells the brain what we need to work on but also helps trigger subtle signals in case we tend to digress from the central topic.

3. We use COLORS throughout. Colors add an extra vibrancy and life to our Mind Map imparting tremendous energy to our Creative Thinking. More importantly, the colors, especially in the context of adults, help calm our mind and focus better. It should, therefore, come as no surprise that there are more than 60,000 plus titles on Amazon.com alone for adult coloring books. In 2015, around 12 million copies of adult coloring books were sold only on Amazon. The huge success of coloring books for adults is testimony to the power of coloring to help us destress and focus better on the issue at hand. I remember while I was presenting this rule in one of my workshops, a participant got up and said "So, you expect us as adults to move around with a pack of crayons in the office?" This is a practical problem and my simple take is that of course the preferred solution is that you have a pack of sharp tipped coloring pens with you, but should this not be

always possible, you can easily procure one of those multicolored ball pens (typically with 4-6 different colored refills) from any good stationary shop or online. This works equally well when you are constrained for time and would like to make a quick Mind Map.

4. We CONNECT our MAIN BRANCHES to the central image. The Main branches represent the first level   or the most important ideas in our Mind Map and are hence thicker than all other branches. As the brain works by association, we must, therefore, further build the Mind Map by connecting the subsequent level of branches stemming from these Main Branches. This leads to radiant hierarchy, which is one of the fundamental foundations of a Mind Map and a very important aspect that both helps improve our understanding of a subject and ignites creative thinking.

5. We use CURVED rather than straight line branches because straight lines are boring for the Brain. You can observe this for yourself. Look around you and if you are sitting in your home, office or any other man-made structure, you will find that you are surrounded by straight lines everywhere. On the other hand, outside in nature, the straight lines are not so easily visible. And what is more pleasing and engaging to the eye? Nature, of course. This is probably also the reason why many small kids find it difficult in their initial years to write between two lines in their text book, or in the process, simply disengage.

6. We use ONE KEY WORD PER LINE to allow the Mind Map greater power and flexibility. You would recall while in school/college, one would highlight few keywords in notes and textbooks. You were in fact unconsciously using this principle by identifying keywords, which would help you recall the complete information set. It is this same principle, which is being used here consciously to identify key words/ideas and knit them together in a more visible manner using Mind Maps. This may appear a little difficult initially for those new to Mind Mapping but with a little practice, it will become easier to identify the keywords.

7. We use IMAGES throughout; remember the adage that an image is worth a thousand words. Given an option to read an autobiographical book of a famous person or to watch a two-hour movie based on the same book, a clear majority of us would probably prefer to watch the movie. This is because the brain thinks through images, but we rarely use this natural propensity while assimilating information or generating ideas. Having said this, I have observed many a times that adults, especially if they have not drawn anything for many years, really find it difficult to start drawing. This is more of a mind block than anything else. The best way to move forward is to start by using simple symbols like a tick mark, a cross sign, an exclamation mark, a smiley, stick figures, arrows etc. Proceeding slowly in this manner, you would soon

graduate to attempting more complex images. If you are not comfortable using images initially, let this not deter you from attempting to make a Mind Map without images. A Mind Map by itself is an image that you are creating even if you do not use images within it.

The above seven principles of Mind Mapping represent in effect the framework for making impactful Mind Maps. Initially when you start your journey with Mind Mapping, you may likely miss out on one or two of the rules therein. Over little time, however, you will master these easily to start making effective Mind Maps. The best part is that Mind Mapping is easy, natural and hence addictive. I commonly observe participants in my workshop getting hooked onto Mind Mapping immediately after having made their first ever Mind Map!

An example of a Mind Map incorporating the aforementioned principles is shared in figure 2.1.

This is personally a very important Mind Map for me since it gave me the courage to quit my 9 to 5 corporate job to pursue my passion for Mind Mapping full time. The Mind Map is inspired by the pain-pleasure principle from Anthony Robbins classic "Awaken the Giant within" [3] (though this Mind Map is software drawn, you would get similar results with a hand drawn one).

The first branch (top right-hand side) captured the Pain that I was trying to avoid by not taking the plunge. The second branch focuses on the current pleasures that were binding me to my present situation. The third branch delved on the pain that I would get if I continued with the

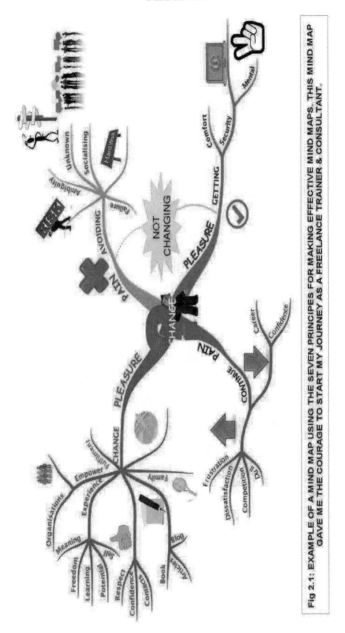

Fig 2.1: EXAMPLE OF A MIND MAP USING THE SEVEN PRINCIPLES FOR MAKING EFFECTIVE MIND MAPS. THIS MIND MAP GAVE ME THE COURAGE TO START MY JOURNEY AS A FREELANCE TRAINER & CONSULTANT.

current situation and finally the fourth branch elaborated all the happiness or pleasure that I could get if I took the plunge. Take a close look at this Mind Map. It may just inspire you to make your's and help you start a new journey!

This is an example of how Mind Maps can help you take critical decisions in life. Though I worked on this map as an individual, it is also easy to use this template for group decision making in an organisational meeting. Now that we have learnt how to make effective individual Mind Maps, let us look at the steps required for using radiant thinking for having mind blowing and engaging meetings.

3. Harnessing Collective Intelligence In Meetings

"Collective Intelligence (CI) is the capacity of human collectives to engage in intellectual cooperation in order to create, innovate & invent"

– Pierre Levy

Before I started using Mind Maps, meetings were just a means to an end. I rarely looked forward to attending or conducting meetings since I always felt that there was something so clinical or inorganic about them, which made them boring. It even never occurred to me to view meetings as a platform where multiple people with unique intelligence met to solve common problems. But one of the biggest challenges that I saw and still observe in many meetings is how to harness that unique thinking process of every individual present so that we discover brilliant and not just work around or evolve workable solutions. It is common to observe in meetings that there is only a certain small percentage of employees, who get engaged with the topic and at the same time trample on the creativity of the other silent attendees. This is the core challenge to be surmounted i.e. how do we harness the unique thinking process of every individual in a meeting to positively contribute to a solution.

Fast forward to a time when I started using Mind Maps in my meetings and I was totally surprised by the immediate positive change in the engagement level of all the participants. It did not take me much time to realize that this was concrete proof that Mind Mapping is the

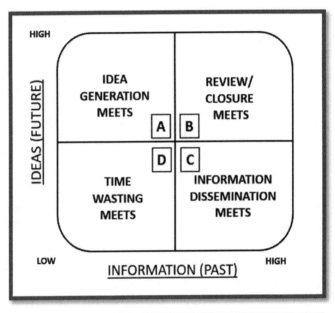

Figure 3.1: A 2 x 2 matrix to understand the various types of meetings in an organisation

natural brain friendly way to work allowing everyone to contribute effortlessly towards the meeting's goals.

Before we go about applying radiant thinking to meetings, let us understand with the help of the two by two matrix (given in figure 3.1) the different type of meetings that usually take place in an organisation.

Every organisational meeting is a combination of ideas generation and information dissemination. When we talk of information, it is something which is already existent, is known and hence in a way is representative of the past. Whereas ideas, on the other hand, represent new possibilities and hence the future. In the figure 3.1, we have Ideas (future) plotted from Low to High on the Y – axis and Information (past) from Low to High on the X-axis.

Let us now take a close look at each of the quadrants.

Quadrant D represents meetings wherein there is a negligible amount of information being disseminated with no or low possibilities of idea generation. These are typically the time wasting and boring meetings, which must either be replaced with other forms of communication (e.g. reports, emails etc.) or revamped completely so that they transit into any of the other quadrants.

The meetings in quadrant C are high on information dissemination and potentially need low Ideas generation. Meetings, which are focused on one sided status reporting, numbers, past performances, key messages etc. come under this category. This many a times is a need felt by an organisation wherein the manager or the leader must present facts and figures, which are complex, long but important and hence the need for a face to face meeting with the attendees. These meetings could even be an end result or an outcome of a previous brainstorming or an ideation meet.

Quadrant B represents meetings, which involve going into the past as well as generating ideas on how to do certain things better in the future. Typically, important review meets, decision making meets and closure meets would fall in this category, which involve an in-depth analysis of past information/facts combined with an identification of new actions for the future.

Quadrant A meetings are the fuel of an organisation, which help to steer it forward and focus more on ideas generation or the future and in the process, help break free from past patterns. Vision meets, brainstorming, problem solving, complex decision making etc. are all part of this very important quadrant.

Now, you would recall that in chapter 1 we saw that Mind Maps in an organisational context help in two important ways

1) Compress large amount of **existing information** in a single page

2) Enhance creative thinking thereby **maximising ideas generation** in various situations:

Do you see the link between these two properties of Mind Mapping and the 2x2 matrix presented earlier? The first property of Mind Maps i.e. to compress large information is useful in meetings falling under categories C and B whereas the ideas generation property of Mind Mapping aids meetings in quadrant A & B.

This takes us to the next question on how to apply Mind Mapping for compressing large amounts of information and for generating ideas.

If your meeting falls in quadrant C i.e. greater focus on information dissemination, you can think about collating your information using a Mind Map. Do ensure that you do follow the instructions for making effective Mind Maps as given in the previous chapter. Once your Mind Map is ready, you can easily use it to present it in your meetings.

This would help in three ways.

First and foremost, once you follow the Mind Mapping approach for information/data presentation, you will realize that you yourself gain much better clarity about your subject. There are many meetings that I have attended wherein it is easy to make out that the level of preparation and/or subject clarity of the meeting coordinator is poor. The audience is easily able to see through the gaps in the presentation.

Second, it will allow for a better understanding of the information presented by the attendees due to the brain friendly nature of Mind Maps, and thirdly, it will act as a bucket for collecting ideas generated during the meeting. Even if you originally thought that this would be purely a data/information presentation meet, you may be surprised by the brilliant ideas that your Mind Map may trigger in the brains of your participants.

So, the steps for category C meetings are quite straightforward, and all of the above factors, will ensure a higher energy level of participation in your meeting.

If your meeting falls in category A or B, it would call for a slightly different approach.

Over a period of time I have realized that there are three important steps for idea generation meets (quadrant A & B) which when followed ensured a much higher level of audience participation in my meetings resulting in better outcomes each instance. To help understand, we look at the application of these steps to a real-life case study [4].

Let me briefly give the background of the case study before going through the three steps.

The case study applies to a leading multinational semiconductor player with an R&D centre in India, comprising over a 1000+ employees, mostly engineers, working in one of the six strategic business units (SBU) of the company. The R&D operations were primarily a cost centre with work being offshored, from outside India, by their parent company. A small sales and marketing team was also maintained at site, which reported to respective SBUs outside India but with minimal interaction with the local R&D teams.

With the maturing of the onsite population, one of the identified challenges was to attract high end work and it was felt that this could happen if the site showcased itself as a leader in innovation. Thus, the need to define and execute a project to improve the innovation culture progressively.

A team of twenty senior managers representing various SBUs and functions was formed to take the project forward. The initial meetings held to define the project goals and macro level objectives posed numerous challenges, some of which were as follows:

a) Diverse Stakeholders: With multiple onsite strategic business units, there existed individual thinking processes aligned more to the respective product lines of their Strategic Business Units rather than to the bigger objective of improving the onsite innovation culture.

b) Low Overall Engagement of Team members: With a team size of twenty, it was very clear that only a few individuals were actively participating whereas the majority either did not seem inclined or was not even getting an opportunity to contribute.

c) Plethora of Ideas: This may seem a contradiction to the challenge mentioned earlier. In fact, the number of ideas and thoughts being thrown were large in number but of low quality since these were coming from a few members only. The ideas generated thus did neither give clear directions to be followed up or actions to be taken.

d) Lack of identification of priorities: Given all the challenges highlighted above, even if actions were identified, it was very difficult to assess which one ought to be taken on a priority basis.

Given the challenges outlined above and the consequent failure of initial meetings, it was imperative to use a different approach to be able to get more clarity in the project goal definition. In consultation with the senior management, it was decided to apply the principles of Radiant thinking via Mind Maps.

This was clearly to be a Quadrant A future focused meeting.

So, against this background and the context provided above, let us look at the three-step process for transforming your meetings completely. (This can be applied to any meeting where there is a strong focus on generating ideas so not just quadrant A but also quadrant B).

Step 1: Tapping Individual Creativity

Once you have identified the meeting topic, there are three possible approaches to follow.

a) You can select a corresponding template from the ones provided in this Book (in the next chapter).

b) You could design your own Mind Map template.

c) You can let the participants design their own templates.

The a) and b) routes are good when the complexity involved is low and there are straight forward defined steps to be followed, or so to say, when the first level branches of the Mind Maps are more or less clear. Approach c) is good when the topic is quite open, and it would be good not to restrict the participants to a specific thinking process at this juncture.

If the participants do not have any knowledge of Mind Mapping, it would be necessary to provide a short introduction explaining the steps for making effective Mind Maps as has been presented in the previous chapter.

Once the participants understand the basics of Mind Mapping, as a first step, they would need to start making their individual Mind Maps on the topic of the meeting. This could be based on the template provided to them by you, or as has been previously indicated, if the topic is broad/open ended, let the individuals design their own template.

To explain by way of an example, if the meeting is about discussing the feasibility of a new project, the template in figure 3.2 [5] can be used. You will find that the Main branches of the Mind Map have been labelled in the template and a brief explanation has been provided about what to expect on the sub-branches of the respective Main branch. Similarly, all the templates provided in this Book have an explanation of the Main branches to guide your Mind Maps. If you are providing your own starting template to the participants, do ensure that you explain your intent for each of the main branches on the template.

As the meeting co-ordinator, you could introduce the participants to the blank template by drawing it on a white board or projecting it on screen or even by taking photocopies of the blank template (minus the comments)

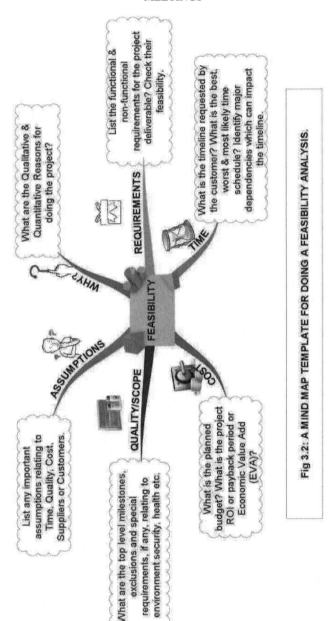

Fig 3.2 : A MIND MAP TEMPLATE FOR DOING A FEASIBILITY ANALYSIS.

and distributing amongst the participants. Use whichever path you find convenient for yourself and the participants to draw their individual Mind Maps.

The meeting participants should use blank pages and colored pens for making their respective Mind Maps. Avoid computer drawn maps at this point unless all the participants are completely comfortable using Mind Mapping Software.

Depending on the complexity of the topic, you can give 15-30 minutes to the participants to draw their Mind Maps. You will be surprised with their speed and attention while Mind Mapping.

In the real-life case study as the topic was quite broad, we encouraged participants to draw their own individual Mind Maps minus any standard template. The steps for making effective Mind Maps were explained along with the problem statement to develop an innovation vision for the organisation with top level goals.

Step 2: Harnessing Collective Intelligence using Radiant Thinking

The next step is a critical one, which is to gather ideas/thoughts of all the participants onto a single Mind Map. As the meeting organiser, you would first require a base Mind Map to start recording the ideas of the participants. The starting point of the base Mind Map is nothing but the initial template, which you have shared with everyone. (In case the participants have their own individual templates, you need to simply start with a blank Mind Map with only the topic written in the centre.)

The very same template can be drawn either on a whiteboard by hand or you could use any of the Mind Mapping Software to project it live on a screen.

Now begin with one of the main branches of your Mind Map and start gathering everyone's ideas. If the group is large, you may follow a structured approach getting everyone to put forth their ideas one by one. Whereas, in case of smaller groups, participation maybe unstructured or free flowing. In either case, you will observe a much higher level of engagement since everyone would have their individual Mind Maps to refer to. Similarly, progress onto the subsequent main branches until you have covered discussing all the branches. Avoid putting up duplicate ideas but do not reject ideas, which may initially seem even a bit crazy. Your focus may be on a specific branch but it is not unusual to get ideas, which may fit well onto other branches. So, feel free to distribute your ideas accordingly.

The first time you do this, you will be surprised by everyone's rapt attention on the base Mind Map, higher engagement via-a-vis the topic, minimal cross talk during the meet, and most of all, an enhanced quality and quantity of ideas generated.

Coming to our real-life case study, a similar process was followed and the ideas being generated by the participants were directly recorded onto a Mind Map on the whiteboard. Once the ideas had been collected from each individual, a draft Mind Map was ready on the board for everyone's reference. This proved to be an extremely valuable anchor, triggering additional ideas from the participants with a lot of energy and enthusiasm. As the exercise progressed, a few themes started emerging, which further helped in the classification of ideas. Once the team felt that all the ideas had been captured on the collective Mind Map, the meeting was concluded.

And the final map, as drawn on the whiteboard as a result of the exercise, is the one presented in figure 3.3. On the face of it, the Mind Map may not look so neat. It was, however, very effective in capturing all the ideas being generated by team members. And we will be able to appreciate the importance of this once we conclude the third step.

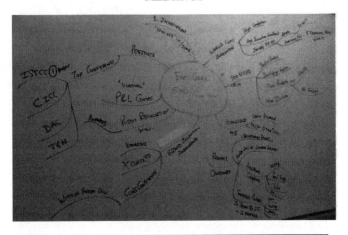

Figure 3.3: The collective group Mind Map made for
the innovation vision & goals

Step 3: Curating the collective intelligence Mind Map

Once all the ideas have been collected on to a single Mind Map, it is necessary to curate it by re-grouping and/or re-classifying the ideas. Though this is best done using software-based Mind Mapping, it can also be done using hand drawn Mind Maps. For our application, we used the iMindMap software. Feel free to use any other Mind Mapping tool that you may be comfortable with. While making the final Mind Map you, however, need to take care of the following:

a) Remove any duplicate ideas that may have crept in.

b) Reorganise the Main branches. If a Mind Map is a clock's face, then it is to be read in a clockwise direction, beginning with 1 o'clock. In other words, the most important main branch will start from 1 o'clock followed by others, moving in a clockwise direction.

c) Feel free to move ideas to more logical branches if they are more closely associated with those rather than the branch on which they may be sitting on presently.

d) Identify qualitative or quantitative goals, which would help define action points to achieve them.

e) Identify action points, wherever emergent, on your Mind Map.

f) Include Images for better engagement with your Mind Map when presenting later.

Once reviewed and redrawn, the Mind Map made using the software emerged as the one given in figure 3.4.

The final vision was captured on the first branch of the Mind Map at 1 o'clock, which was to create an innovation culture to demonstrate the high competence of the employees, instil a passion for innovation combined with a strong commitment to innovation from all, beginning with the management.

A quick word on the other branches in this important Mind Map.

It became clear for the very first time that there were distinct themes for which effort would have to be put in for building a culture of innovation. The first branch "Sales" captured the sales team's need for support from the SBUs for India (i.e. local) centric innovative products in the health and energy sector. There was also an

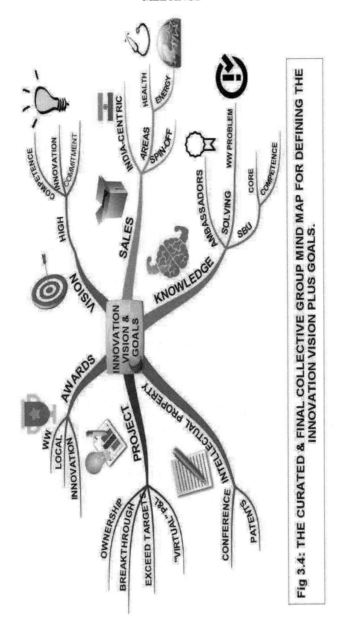

Fig 3.4: THE CURATED & FINAL COLLECTIVE GROUP MIND MAP FOR DEFINING THE INNOVATION VISION PLUS GOALS.

ambitious goal of one such product leading to a Spin Off. The "Knowledge" branch captured the need to create experts inside the SBUs, who could contribute to solving technical problems beyond local operations while focussing on their respective SBUs core competence. Enhancing the "Intellectual Property" portfolio through increased technical paper submissions to prestigious conferences and patent filing was another important area to work in. Keeping the focus on the local project development environment helped capture the need to develop a mentality to exceed end targets and look for breakthroughs. Participation in various industry "awards" was identified as another important theme to be able to benchmark the organisation's innovation culture against other leading industry players.

Once these areas had been identified, the next step was to form sub-committees around each of the themes and identify a leader for each. With the sub-committees in place, it was now easier to identify the goals for the respective areas. Thus, with the help of radiant thinking, finally there was clarity about the project goals to be achieved for building a culture of innovation. This in fact eventually led to several achievements, including launch of an internal conference, increased patent filings, multiple industry recognitions for innovation, new local market centric products development etc.

The collective Mind Map helps organise a large amount of information or ideas together and acts as a seed for curating a bigger creation and its implementation. Just as a seed requires constant nourishment, the Mind Map calls for sustained focus and energy to have the desired positive impact.

Now that you have been through the three steps for conducting effective and engaging meetings using Mind Maps, you are now ready to start using the templates in this Book or even create your own.

You would have realized by now that Mind Mapping is an easy to use and simple technique to clarify one's thinking and generate new thoughts. In fact, all functions in an organisation can benefit from the usage of radiant thinking via Mind Maps.

The next chapter comprises a wide variety of templates relevant for various important functions in an organisation, which are categorised below.

1. GOALS SETTING: Relevant for all, right from the Top Management to the most junior in hierarchy. The visual aspect of Mind Maps not only helps clarify goals but also triggers the much-desired motivation to achieve them.

2. DECISION MAKING: An organization is only as good as its decision making process. Why not strengthen it further with brain friendly Mind Mapping templates as included in this section?

3. COMMUNICATION: Communication is critical within every organization, whether it is one to one between the employees or a one to many from the leadership. In either situation, a Mind Maps helps in achieving a high level of clarity in one's thought process,

which is the most important precursor to communication via any media.

4. PLANNING: Effective planning is again a skill that is required across any organization's hierarchy, the context and dimension of which may vary. Discover with the Planning Mind Map templates on how you can excel at Business Planning, Strategic planning, or even weekly planning.

5. SALES & MARKETING: The critical revenue generating engine of any organization can "profit" much more by transforming some of their existing techniques into a Mind Map format as would be evident from the templates included for this section.

6. PROJECT MANAGEMENT: A project is about a new "creation" of a product/service but managing projects demands "creativity". Get that extra dash of creativity for your project teams with the Mind Map templates included for managing projects better.

7. INNOVATION: is the celebration and culmination of creativity. Mind Mapping not only helps ignite organizational creativity, but more importantly, helps transform it into innovation for commercial success. Check out how with the help of the Innovation templates.

The above are broadly all the important areas, which improved upon, would help any organisation evolve multiple dimensions. So, start working with the template which appears closest to the topic for your meet. Each of the branches of the template has been further explained, which you may use both for yourself as well as for communicating with your team (remember step 1, help your team make the individual mind maps using the corresponding template).

Do not panic if you don't find a Mind Map template corresponding to your need. Simply drop me an email at maneesh.dutt@outlook.com and I will do whatever I can to help you out!

An organisation thrives only when it can harness the collective intelligence of each and every of its unique employees. Radiant thinking via Mind Maps is the perfect platform to ignite multiple individuals to direct their creativity cumulatively into a single subject. You don't have to believe me! Simply start experimenting with the templates provided in this Book and let the results surprise you.

On that note, keep Mind Mapping, keep learning and feel free to share with me thoughts (or better still Mind Maps!!) at any point at maneesh.dutt@outlook.com.

4. Ready To Use Templates For Various Meeting

"You don't have to be genius or a visionary or a college graduate to be successful. You just need a framework & a dream"

– Michael Dell

Depending on the type of meeting that you would like to conduct, you can locate the closest template from those provided here. Simply use that template as a starting framework to harness the collective intelligence of your team for a successful meeting.

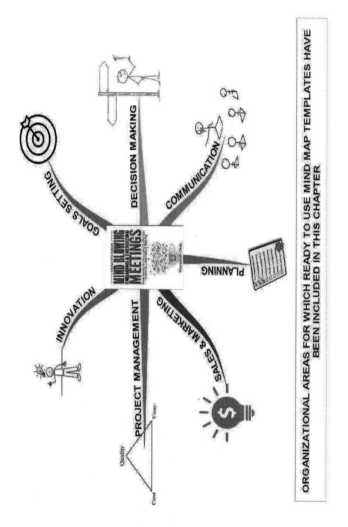

GOALS SETTING

DECISION MAKING

COMMUNICATION

INNOVATION

PROJECT MANAGEMENT

Quality

Time

Cost

SALES & MARKETING

PLANNING

MIND BLOWING MEETINGS

ORGANIZATIONAL AREAS FOR WHICH READY TO USE MIND MAP TEMPLATES HAVE BEEN INCLUDED IN THIS CHAPTER

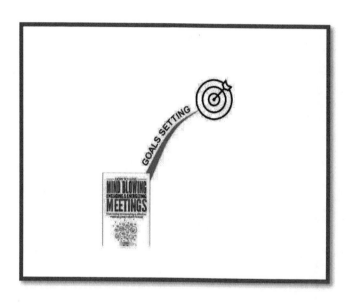

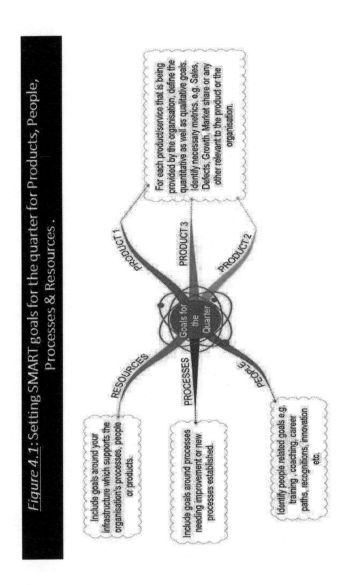

Figure 4.1: Setting SMART goals for the quarter for Products, People, Processes & Resources.

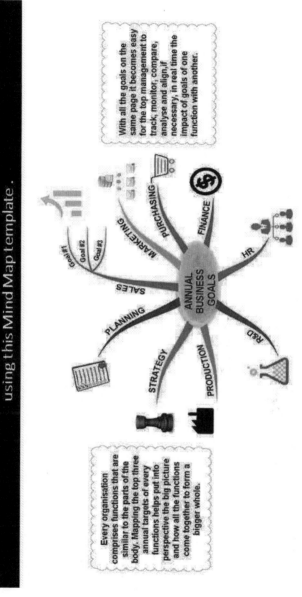

Figure 4.2: Stitching the annual business goals of all functions together using this Mind Map template .

With all the goals on the same page it becomes easy for the top management to track, monitor, compare, analyse and align,if necessary, in real time the impact of goals of one function with another.

Every organisation comprises functions that are similar to the parts of the body. Mapping the top three annual targets of every functions helps put into perspective the big picture and how all the functions come together to form a bigger whole.

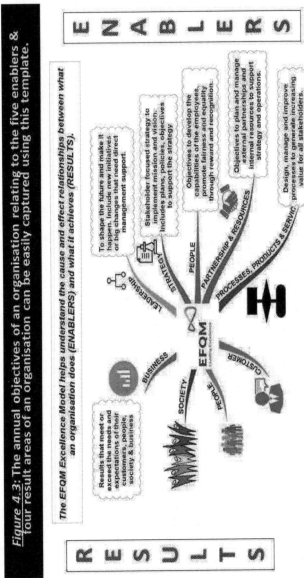

Figure 4.3: The annual objectives of an organisation relating to the five enablers & four result areas of an organisation can be easily captured using this template.

The EFQM Excellence Model helps understand the cause and effect relationships between what an organisation does (ENABLERS) and what it achieves (RESULTS).

Ref: "An Overview of the EFQM Excellence model" available at http://www.efqm.org/the-efqm-excellence-model

Reference [6]

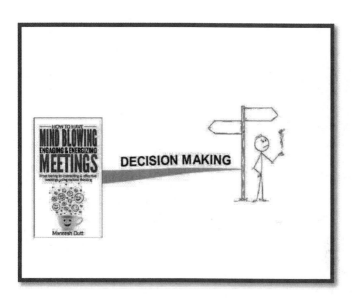

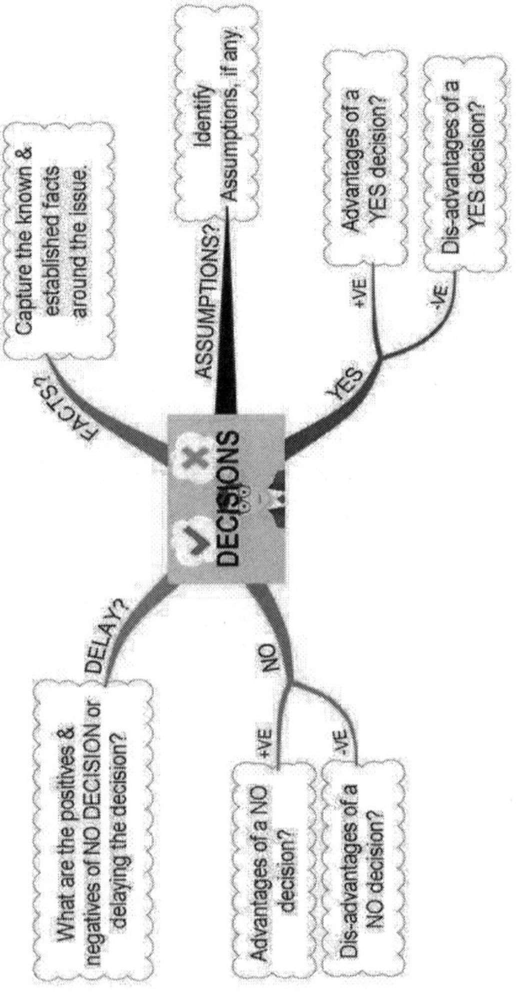

Figure 4.4: Analysing a YES-NO decision in a complex situation using the above template will help gain added clarity for good decision making.

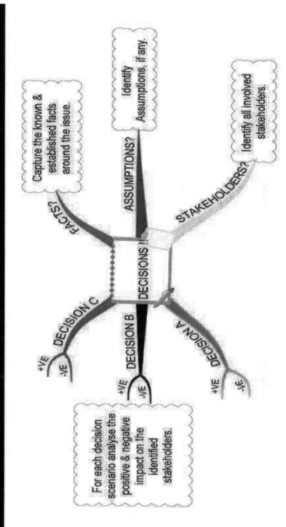

Figure 4.5: Decision making template to analyse impact of alternative decisions and help aid choosing the right one.

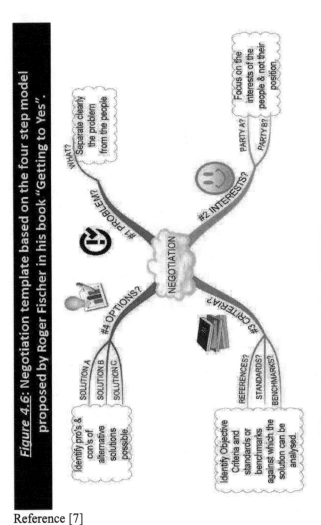

Figure 4.6: Negotiation template based on the four step model proposed by Roger Fischer in his book "Getting to Yes".

Reference [7]

Ref: R. Fischer and W. Ury, Getting to Yes, New York: Penguin Books, 1991.

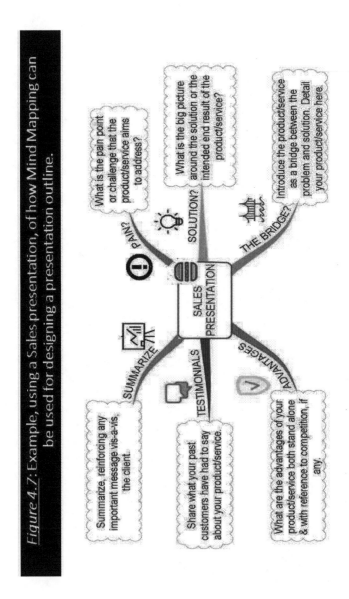

Figure 4.7: Example, using a Sales presentation, of how Mind Mapping can be used for designing a presentation outline.

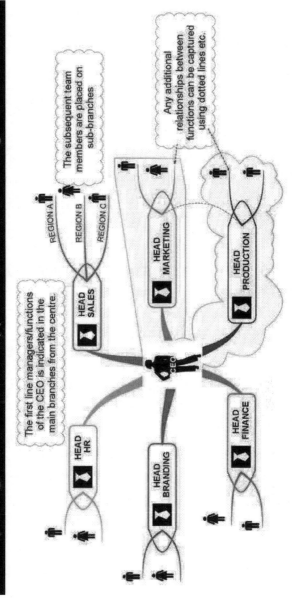

Figure 4.8: An Organisation represented as a radiant hierarchy using Mind Maps as against the traditional pyramid structure of an organisation chart.

The subsequent team members are placed on sub-branches

Any additional relationships between functions can be captured using dotted lines etc.

The first line managers/functions of the CEO is indicated in the main branches from the centre.

REGION A
REGION B
REGION C

HEAD SALES

HEAD MARKETING

HEAD PRODUCTION

CEO

HEAD HR

HEAD BRANDING

HEAD FINANCE

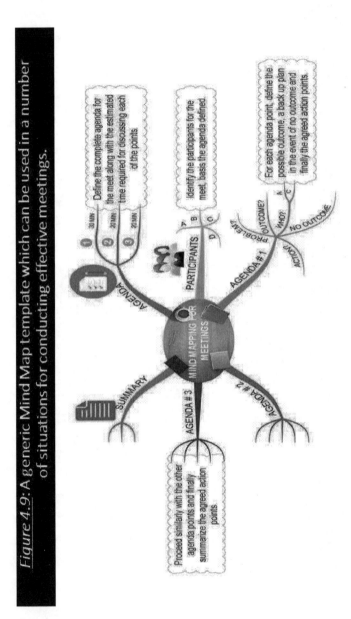

Figure 4.9: A generic Mind Map template which can be used in a number of situations for conducting effective meetings.

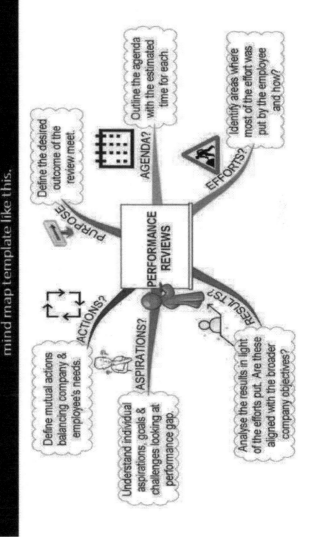

Figure 4.10: An effective performance review can be conducted using a mind map template like this.

63

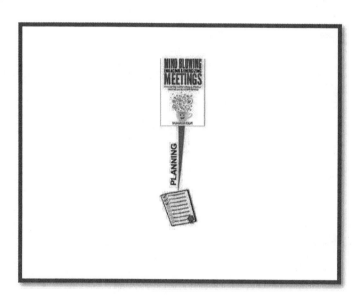

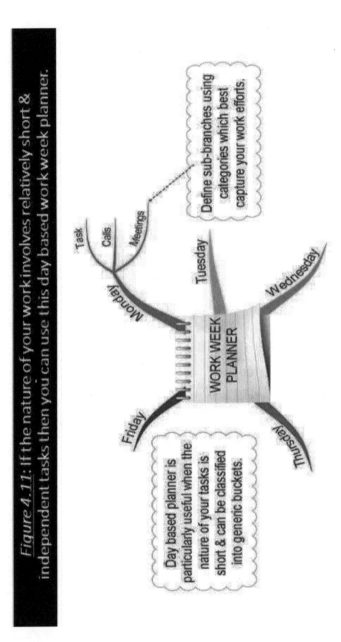

Figure 4.11: If the nature of your work involves relatively short & independent tasks then you can use this day based work week planner.

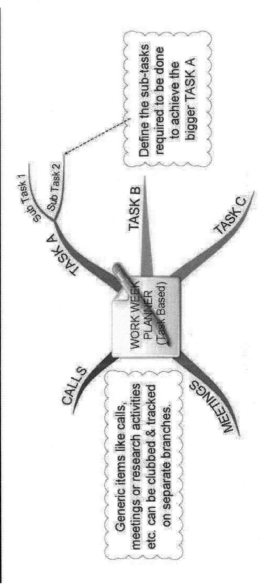

Figure 4.12: A Task Based weekly planner template, as shown, can be used if you work involves longer duration tasks with multiple sub tasks.

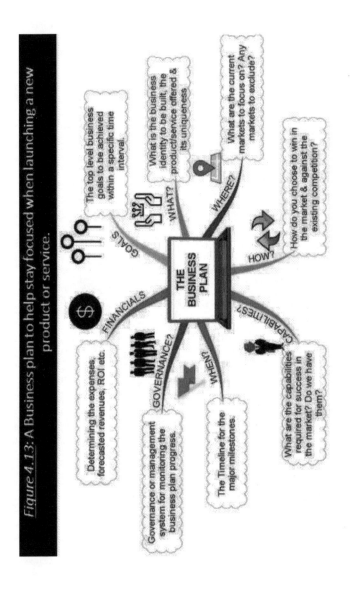

Figure 4.13: A Business plan to help stay focused when launching a new product or service.

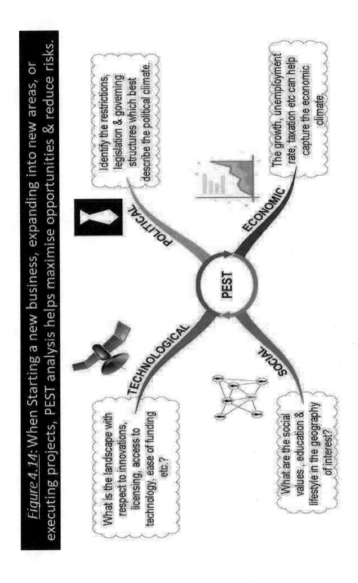

Figure 4.14: When Starting a new business, expanding into new areas, or executing projects, PEST analysis helps maximise opportunities & reduce risks.

Figure 4.15: Use this FABV template to effectively sell any product/service by focusing on its features, their advantages, benefit to the customer & the value.

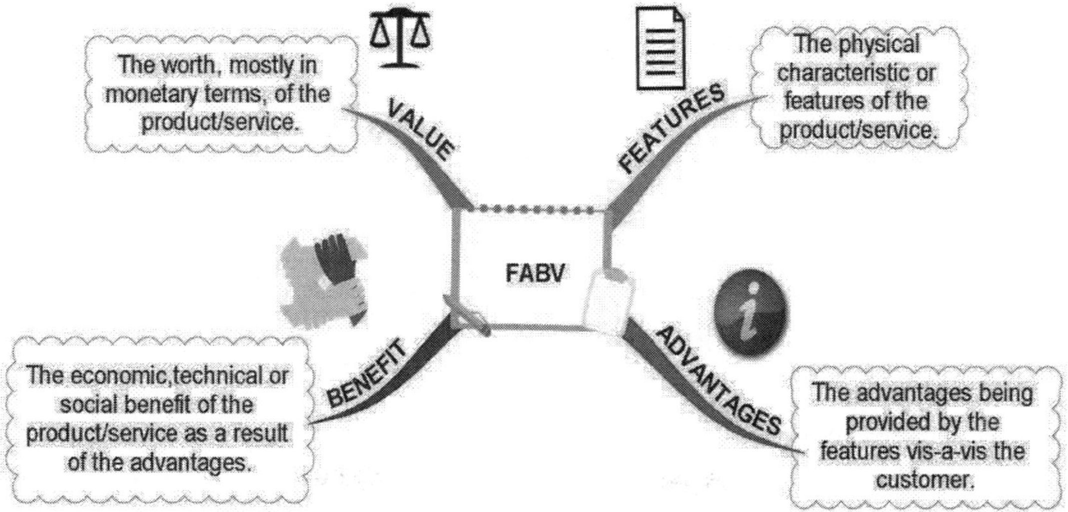

FEATURES — The physical characteristic or features of the product/service.

ADVANTAGES — The advantages being provided by the features vis-a-vis the customer.

VALUE — The worth, mostly in monetary terms, of the product/service.

BENEFIT — The economic, technical or social benefit of the product/service as a result of the advantages.

FABV

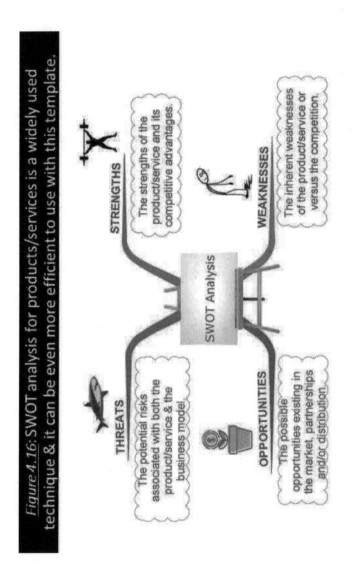

Figure 4.16: SWOT analysis for products/services is a widely used technique & it can be even more efficient to use with this template.

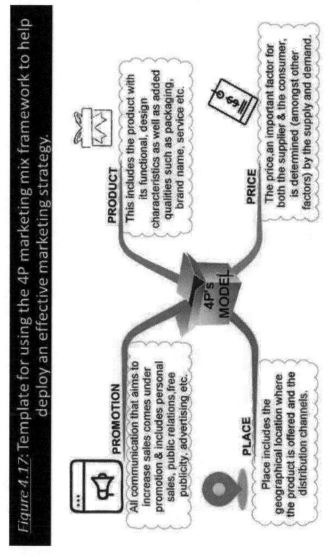

Figure 4.17: Template for using the 4P marketing mix framework to help deploy an effective marketing strategy.

Reference [8]

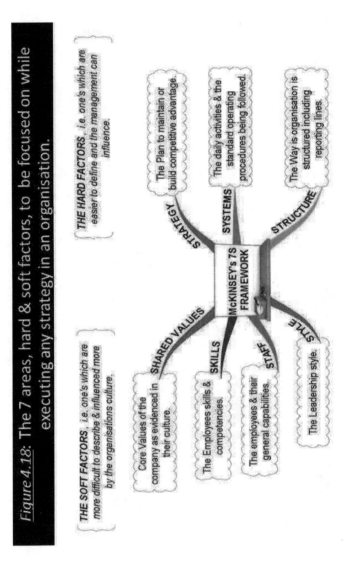

Figure 4.18: The 7 areas, hard & soft factors, to be focused on while executing any strategy in an organisation.

THE HARD FACTORS, i.e. one's which are easier to define and the management can influence.

THE SOFT FACTORS, i.e. one's which are more difficult to describe & influenced more by the organisations culture.

McKINSEY's 7S FRAMEWORK

STRATEGY — The Plan to maintain or build competitive advantage.

SYSTEMS — The daily activities & the standard operating procedures being followed.

STRUCTURE — The Way is organisation is structured including reporting lines.

SHARED VALUES — Core Values of the company as evidenced in their culture.

SKILLS — The Employees skills & competencies.

STAFF — The employees & their general capabilities.

STYLE — The Leadership style.

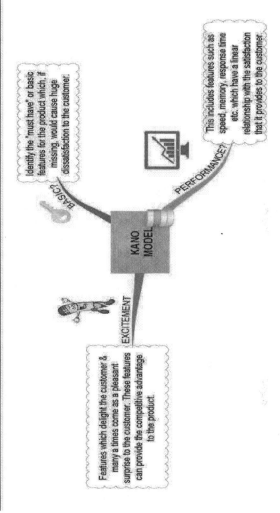

Figure 4.19: Using this template KANO's model can be easily applied to any product/service to prioritise its features by its impact on the end user.

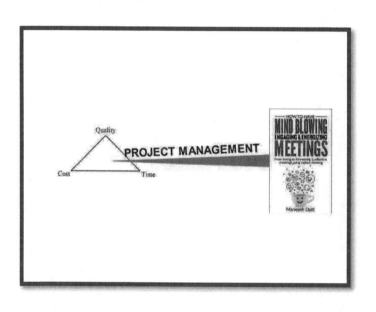

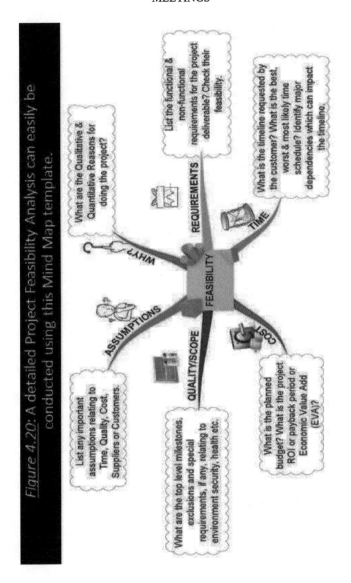

Figure 4.20: A detailed Project Feasibility Analysis can easily be conducted using this Mind Map template.

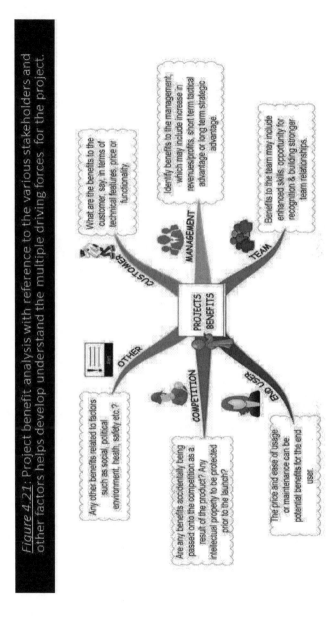

Figure 4.21: Project benefit analysis with reference to the various stakeholders and other factors helps develop understand the multiple driving forces for the project.

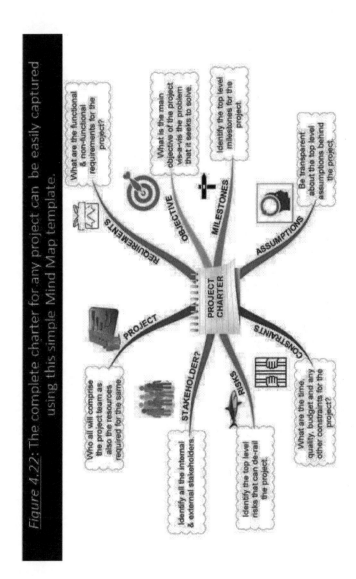

Figure 4.22: The complete charter for any project can be easily captured using this simple Mind Map template.

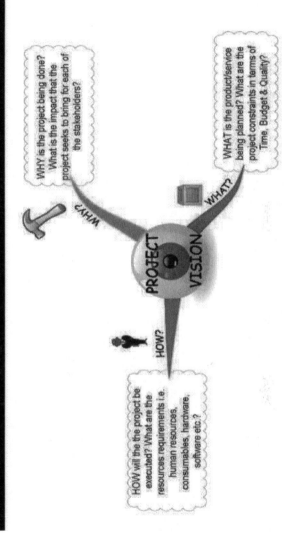

Figure 4.23: A simple Mind Map template like this can help articulate any project's vision with a lot of clarity.

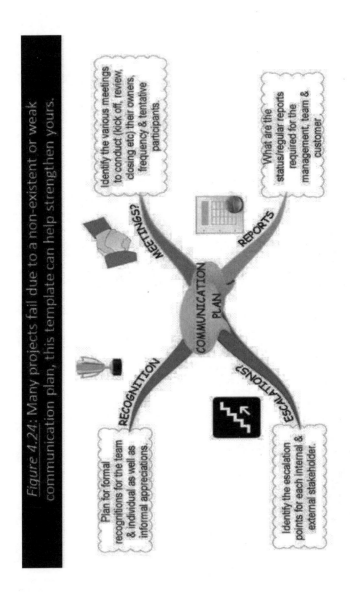

Figure 4.24: Many projects fail due to a non-existent or weak communication plan, this template can help strengthen yours.

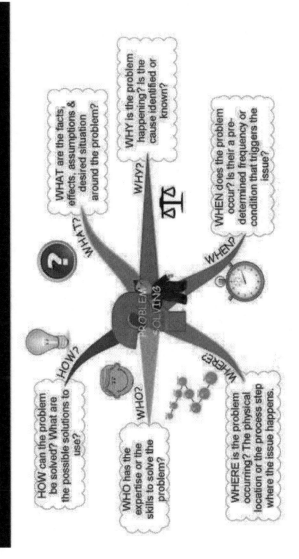

Figure 4.25: Problem Analysis & Solving Using the 5W and 1H technique.

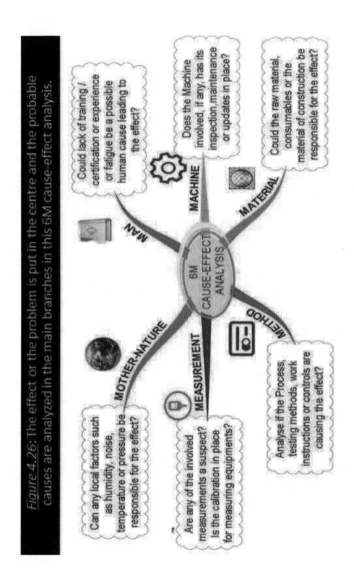

Figure 4.26: The effect or the problem is put in the centre and the probable causes are analyzed in the main branches in this 6M cause-effect analysis.

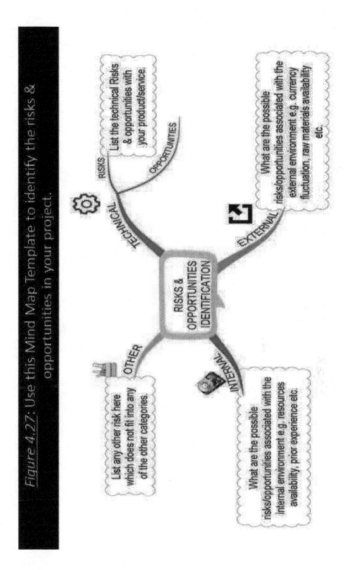

Figure 4.27: Use this Mind Map Template to identify the risks & opportunities in your project.

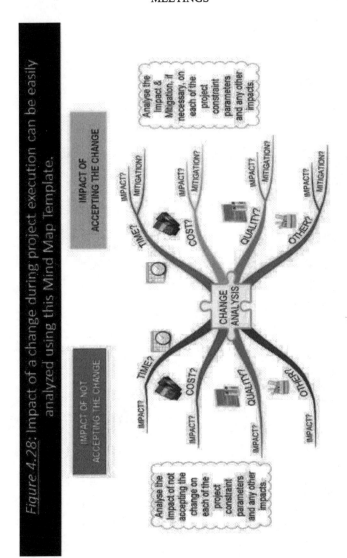

Figure 4.28: Impact of a change during project execution can be easily analyzed using this Mind Map Template.

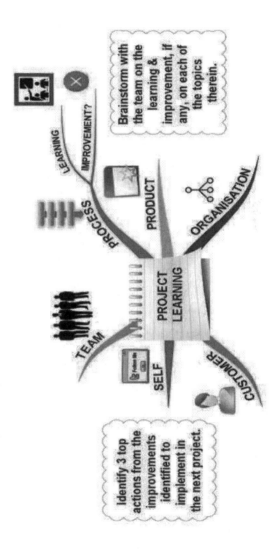

Figure 4.29: This mind map template can be used for facilitating a project learning meet on project closure.

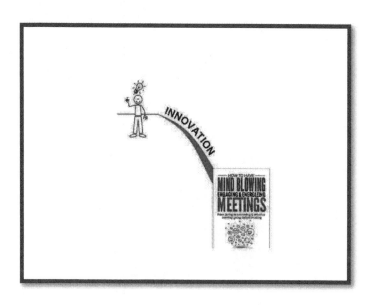

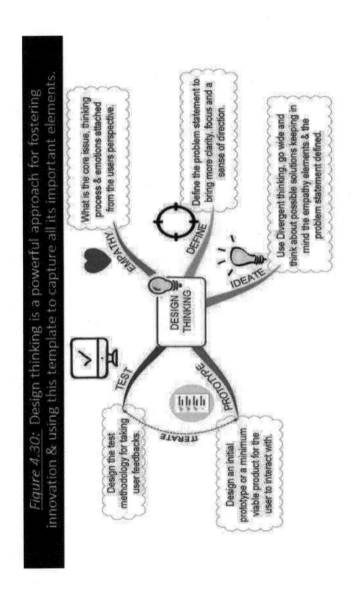

Figure 4.30: Design thinking is a powerful approach for fostering innovation & using this template to capture all its important elements.

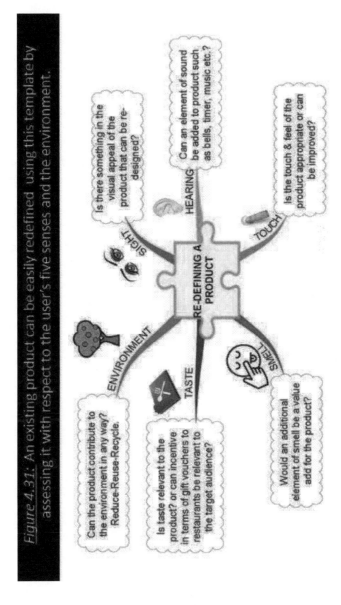

Figure 4.31: An existing product can be easily redefined using this template by assessing it with respect to the user's five senses and the environment.

Additional Resources To Keep You Going...

The following additional resources will be helpful to keep you motivated in your journey towards becoming a Mind Mapping expert:

✓ Interested in a soft copy of a specific Mind Map templates (in iMindmap format), included in this book? Simply email me at maneesh.dutt@outlook.com referring to the figure number of the of the Mind Map template.

✓ Check out *free Mind Map learning videos* available on my website at https://maneeshdutt.com/resources/.

✓ Subscribe to www.maneeshdutt.com for receiving *articles on Mind Mapping*.

✓ Subscribe to the Biggest Mind Map Library - www.biggerplate.com *– to access the best of the*

Mind Maps being contributed from across the globe.

✓ Those interested in *Software driven Mind Mapping* can download the trial version of iMindMap at https://imindmap.com/software/

✓ Book a *complimentary 1-hour seminar/webinar* for your institution/company by filling in the request form at http://maneeshdutt.com/consultancy-speaking/

✓ Interested in Mind Mapping for Project Management? Then this book could be useful https://amzn.to/2IiRKcF or you could also attend an online course on Udemy here https://bit.ly/2uGGG0Y

✓ If self-help using Mind Maps and coloring is what you are looking for to bring you closer towards understanding your life goals and indeed realize them, then this is the book for you https://amzn.to/2rpnTFX

✓ If you are struggling – either as a parent or a teacher - to teach kids, then learn more about how Mind Maps can help you through this book: https://amzn.to/2FS0jFU or the online course on UDEMY here https://bit.ly/2KxUi7N

GET A 30% DISCOUNT ON PURCHASE OF BOOKS

& ON TRAININGS ON THE AUTHOR'S WEBSITE

WWW.MANEESHDUTT.COM

USE THE COUPON CODE AT CHECKOUT*:

READER30

(*: Valid only for readers in India)

Reactions To Other Books By The Author

MIND MAPS FOR ORGANISATIONS

"Tony Buzan created a worldwide phenomenon with Mind Maps, but as with any revolutionary system that explores human thought, subsequent interpretations can often prove less insightful. Fortunately, Mind Maps for Effective Project Management by Maneesh Dutt bucks this trend to deliver an authoritative and clearly presented guide to unleashing their potential...."

- Spotlight Review, Bookviral.com

"...I highly respect Maneesh as a trainer, for setting out to help others enhance their creativity, and for taking the risk and quitting his previous job to be able to do so in the first place..."

- Chris Griffiths, Founder and CEO of OpenGenius, the parent company of ThinkBuzan, Best-selling author, GRASP The Solution

"... Our process-oriented industries need more creativity... so it is definitely worth investing some time to evaluate this book and its thesis for yourself!" *-Manas Fuloria, Co-founder and CEO, Nagarro*

"...Maneesh has written a compelling thesis and is a must read for CXOs and project managers alike, to get the most out of projects!" *-Sameer Garde, ex-President, South Asia, Philips India*

"...the initiative by Maneesh is a welcome and valuable contribution. This is especially useful for mid-level and senior people but can be used by all age groups." *-Tushar Bhatia, Founder & CEO, EmpXtrack*

Readers Reactions:

"Excellent book! Was amazed to see how a seemingly simple looking 'synapses' can actually untangle tough real-life situations!"

"A must read for people who are in the business of PM and innovation."

"Most comprehensive handbook of project management"

MIND MAPS FOR SELF-HELP

"When focusing deeply on a simple task, other anxieties become less present, less pervasive, allowing for greater clarity of thought and this is the principle that underpins Dutt's Live Life Colourfully. Readers familiar with Dutt's previous release, Mind Maps for Effective Project Management will be in no doubt as to depth and breadth of knowledge he brings to the subject and here he shares another powerful tool for turning great ideas into a functional reality."

- Spotlight Review, Bookviral.com

"Dutt's book is a beginner's guide to the potent tool that enables one to unlock his or her creative thinking prowess" — ***Punya Srivastava, Associate Editor, Life Positive***

Readers Reactions:

"The book is great, I just learnt so much from it. I can see outside the box, clear thinking, how to Mind Map with colorful Mandalas. Maneesh Dutt has easily explained the Mind Map techniques in a fun and relaxed way."

"A wonderful approach to unwind yourself by way of coloring and thereby overcome stress."

"A must book to read, easy to understand with deep positive impact."

"Maneesh is a vivid writer. He has created the right amalgamation of mandalas and mind mapping, helping structured thinking and pragmatic approach. A very useful tool in decision making and a highly recommended read."

"Great book - very helpful in setting goals. Perfect Christmas gift."

MIND MAPS FOR EMPOWERING TEACHERS & PARENTS ALIKE

It is easy for a child to ensure laser like focus while playing or when engaged in something of his/her interest. A child does not need to learn to concentrate and focus. He is a natural at it! The real problem statement is, therefore, not how to increase a child's ability to concentrate. It is in fact how to revolutionize our teaching methodologies to match the energy and enthusiasm of a child. This is what the book is all about.

"Working as compact guide, this book offers techniques which enable a child to move from a low understanding-low memory zone to a high understanding-high memory zone in the understanding-memory quadrant. Dutt's book

gets my recommendation" – ***Punya Srivastava, Associate Editor, Life-Positive Magazine****.*

<u>*Readers Reactions:*</u>

"Mind Maps for kids is an awesome tool to help them get focused."

"Happily recommending this book to students."

"Life altering techniques in child teaching methodology"

"…I only wish if somebody thought me in this way in School."

"…. the book has helped a lot, I'd say that the book will surely reach out to a bigger crowd and influence more students' minds".

"Very impressive and must buy book for young Indian parents"

"It is great reading, simple language and focus on main content rather on stories. I would highly recommend this book for parents."

About The Author

Maneesh is a Chemical engineer from IIT-D and an MBA by qualification. He is a Tony Buzan Licensed Instructor for Mind Maps and trained by the inventor of Mind Maps himself, Mr. Tony Buzan.

He has made it his mission to take Mind Maps to all interested and is a sought-after consultant and trainer on Mind Maps, Creativity, Innovation and Project Management. His subject is sector agnostic and as a result of which he has clients from across industries ranging from Pharmaceutical to Airlines to IT to Automotive etc. etc. He loves to express himself through his writings and has a wide variety of other interests, which include project management, writing poems, Reiki healing and numerology.

He can be contacted at maneesh.dutt@outlook.com

Acknowledgments

Many years ago, I embarked upon my tentative journey of applying Mind Maps in various situations. The initial curiosity to apply Mind Maps slowly transformed into a passion to use Mind Maps every day in every situation.

I am, therefore, first of all indebted to Mr. Tony Buzan, inventor of Mind Maps, for igniting my neurons with this amazing tool.

Now having conducted workshops across sectors on Mind Maps for so many years, I would like to extend my heartfelt thanks to all the participants in my programs for helping me delve deeper into the subject. My conviction in this tool has grown thanks to the extremely encouraging feedback received from so many of you.

In fact, on a related note, one of the primary reasons prompting me to write this Book has been the constant feedback I have received from a number of workshop participants and senior managers on the need for a management book, which could help institutionalise Mind Maps on a wider scale across hierarchy and functions. I realize that a "Meeting" is something, which touches everyone within an organisation and hence this Book that can hopefully provide an answer or be the tool for driving application of Mind Maps in organisations on a larger scale.

ACKNOWLEDGEMENTS

Having said that, I wish to share that I have used a lot of practical management experiences in this Book gathered over the two decades that I worked with various organisations. And I have been exceptionally fortunate to have had bosses, who coached and cared for me during my years in various corporate organisations. A good amount of learning was acquired while interacting with them and whatever success I have achieved in reaching my goals is thanks to their grooming and nurturing.

I would sincerely like to thank all the readers of all my books. There is no way that I could have ventured this far as to publish this fourth book of mine without your motivating reviews.

I would also like to acknowledge the wonderful efforts being put in by Liam Hughes, Founder, www.biggerplate.com, for consistently spreading positive and practical news about the potential of Mind Mapping across the globe. Your work is an immense inspiration for all fellow Mind Mappers across the globe.

My sincere thanks to Aparna Sharma for her usual impeccable edits of my books and for constantly amazing me with the breadth of her expertise in editing a varied range of subjects.

My sincere gratitude and thanks to my parents, Mr. Sudarshan Lal Dutt and Mrs. Shalila Dutt, for helping me grow in an ever loving and learning environment in my formative years.

ACKNOWLEDGEMENTS

Finally, a big and a very special thanks to my wife Seema and our twins, Kaamya and Krish-- without your support, none of my books would have ever seen the light of day. Your thoughtfulness towards ensuring that I always get the space required for penning my books is really commendable and has been the foundation of my writing career.

Bibliography

[1] T. Buzan, How To Mind Map, London: Thorsons, 2002.

[2] T. Buzan and B. Buzan, The Mind Map Book, Great Britain: BBC Active, 2010.

[3] A. Robbins, Awaken The Giant Within, London: Simon & Schuster UK Ltd., 1991.

[4] M. Dutt, "Enabling Project Teams with Radiant Thinking," in Project Management Practioners Conference (PMI), Bangalore, 2017.

[5] M. Dutt, Mind Maps for Effective Project Management, Chennai, INDIA: Notion Press, 2015.

[6] EFQM, "An Overview of the EFQM Excellence model"," European Foundation for Quality Management, 2018. [Online]. Available: http://www.efqm.org/the-efqm-excellence-model. [Accessed Jun 2018].

[7] R. Fisher and W. Ury, Getting to Yes, New York: Penguin Books, 1991.

BIBLIOGRAPHY

[8] J. McCarthy, "Marketing mix 4P's," Tools Hero, 2017. [Online]. Available: https://www.toolshero.com/marketing/marketing-mix-4p-mccarthy/.

Testimonials

TESTIMONIALS FROM PARTCIPANTS TO MANEESH DUTT's WORKSHOP

"Session was very good and by using this we can find solution to various problems. Mr. Maneesh is a very good presenter, he customized the presentation as per pharma industry and also designed the topic in a way to give maximum benefit to the participants" - Sandipan Roy, *Sun Pharma*

"The course content and the way of presentation was excellent. The exercises were quite good" -Nirmal Kumar Parida, *Samsung*

"Very Interesting!! Eye Opener!! Mind Opener!!" - Hemali Bhutani Mahajan, *Genesis Burson Marsteller*

"After a long time new thing to learn which will definitely help to enhance my skills. A must have training session for everyone" - Rahul Sharma, *Saigun Technologies Pvt. Ltd.*

Great Concept, Great activities, exercises, Very Engaging Content. Can be practically applied to a lot of situations. Maneesh is very knowledgeable, engaged very well with everyone, was approachable, answered all questions very well & clearly explained concepts. - Ratnabali Banerjee, *Innodata*

"The session was wonderful. The topic, was well covered, examples made the learning well grasped and the exercises made us cut the grey areas. Maneesh delivered the entire training session flawlessly. Thorough knowledge, deep understanding of the content ended up with flawless delivery" - Manish Kumar, *IL& FS Energy Development Co. Ltd*

"Very informative background on Mind Maps. The basics cleared quite a few issues for me while creating Mind Maps. Maneesh is very knowledgeable on the subject of Mind Maps. He clearly explained the concepts while keeping the entire session very interesting."- Rashik Kathuria, *Rashik Kathuria Consulting*.

Excellent Way of shaping thoughts into workable ideas. The depth of coverage was apt and various exercises supported in comprehending the topic being taught in a better way. Maneesh has a flair for training, is knowledgeable and has been able to share the concepts, ideas in a serene manner. - Chander Shekhar Sharma, *DHFL Pramerica*

This was a new subject and I learnt to look at creativity and mind. Maneesh was excellent and very good with his subject. - Ravindra Singh, *Air India Ltd.*

Absolutely amazing, I was doing research on it and found the session to clear many of my doubts. Amazing exercises. - Subhash Chand, *Serpholic Media Pvt. Ltd.*

A brilliant session which has opened some clogged pores to learning better through the tool of Mind Maps which will make learning far more interactive, doable, creative and everlasting. It has given words to my thoughts!! - Seema Sahay, Principal, *G.D.Goenka Public School, Sarita Vihar*

Good teaching method. Got overall clarity on the subject. Will practice often in resolving problems and new projects. - Kaushik Manna, *Rockman Industries*.

For more testimonials please visit: *https://maneeshdutt.com/clients-and-testimonial/*

35745784R10071

Made in the USA
San Bernardino, CA
14 May 2019